WORKBOOK
FOR

COMPLEX

PTSD

FROM SURVIVING TO THRIVING

BY
PETE WALKER

WRIGHT PUBLISHERS

Table of Contents

HOW TO USE THIS WORKBOOK

The reader is to use this workbook as a blueprint or a recovery map from childhood trauma, abuse, emotional abandonment, and every challenge that can be linked to CPTSD.

Each chapter is a journey.

Take your time to digest all you've read. As you read, reflect on your life and the places you need healing. If you do, even though it may take time, you'll begin to see healing and progress in the right places.

You can go through each of the topics and find the chapter most appealing to you in order to determine the order in which you will be reading this book. Don't worry, each chapter can stand alone so you wouldn't be missing out on anything.

P.S. I don't advise that you use this workbook just once. You need to use, reuse and come back to it. The reason is that healing and recovery aren't a one-time thing. It's progressive and in steps. That's why you need to come back to what you've learned.

CHAPTER SUBDIVISIONS

Each chapter comprises 6 different sections

1. Summary: An overview of the chapter designed to help you remember its essence and what you learned in each chapter of "COMPLEX PTSD: From Surviving to Thriving." Use this as a quick recap of what the chapter discusses.
2. Key takeaways: These are the salient points to take note of in each chapter. Basically, if you don't remember anything else in the chapter, remember these.
3. Lessons: Salient teachings to put into practice in your day-to-day living. You can call them takeaway tips to improve the relevant areas in your life. You can discuss these with friends or anyone walking with you on this journey to rid yourself of trauma.
4. Goals: This encapsulates what each chapter aims to achieve for the reader, and as a part of the larger book.
5. Action plans: Curated steps to take in reaching your goals on the way to thriving. While these have been highlighted with care, it is recommended that you identify personal action plans as you read. These will be a custom map to recovery made just for you.
6. Questions: This is where you make sure or confirm that the previous 5 steps have not been read in vain. Answering some of the questions will lead you to ask more personal questions that will aid your journey to recovery from Complex PTSD.

Stay true to these 6 steps to kickstart your Healing Journey.

INTRODUCTION

Complex PTSD by Pete Walker is written to help you heal from inadequate childhood love and emotional abandonment which many of us suffer from. It is a blueprint or a map that you can engage to heal from your childhood wounds.

You may find out that some of the points are repeated more than once or twice; it is the best way to emphasize the great importance of engaging the themes of recovery work that's essential to you and your growth.

It's understandable if you feel lost while reading. This happens because your inner child can connect with what is written so your present self may initially find out there's something rumbling within. To find yourself, remember that the book is a map with themes. Use the theme of the chapter you're reading as a key to reconnecting.

The goal of this book is recovery from CPTSD. If that's what you want, you can be sure that that's what you'll get.

Who should use this workbook?

This book is for everyone who is a survivor of childhood trauma, abuse, abandonment, toxic shame, fear, blame, and your inner critic. If you grew up in a dysfunctional family or if you had parents who made life unbearable for you as a child or now that you're an adult, you should use this workbook.

If you know someone who falls under the category in the previous paragraph, please get them a copy.

What's in it for me and why is it important

This book is a multimodal treatment approach to CPTSD. It is oriented towards the most prevalent kind of CPTSD, the kind that comes from growing up in a severely abusive and/or negative family.

The book describes a journey of healing the damage that occurs when you suffer traumatizing abuse and abandonment.

Everyone deserves to live happily and have a beautiful life devoid of mental or emotional trauma. That's why this book was written and that's what you'll get when you read it.

Your past may be filled with pain and horrors from your childhood but your future can be truly beautiful. However, the future is built on the past. This means you need to be free from your past and make peace with it to have a good future.

This is why this book is important. It is by carefully cooperating with this book that you'll be able to relive your past and face your future with no fear, emotionally and mentally strong so you can be all you want to be with no exceptions and excuses.

PART 1: AN OVERVIEW OF RECOVERING

CHAPTER 1: THE JOURNEY OF RECOVERING FROM CPTSD

Summary

What is complex CPTSD?

C is for complex and PTSD stands for Post-Traumatic Stress Disorder. CPTSD is a more severe form of PTSD. It involves five troubling features which are:

i.   Emotional flashbacks: the most obvious feature. It comes with painful emotional flashbacks without a visual component. There's an overwhelming feeling of being abused/abandoned and it comes with depression, shame, fear, grief, rage, and alienation while triggering your fight/flight instinct.

ii.   Toxic shame: replaces the survivor's self-esteem with an overwhelming sense that the survivor is fatally flawed, loathsome, stupid, and ugly. It brings back overwhelming self-disdain to the way the survivor felt when suffering the contempt and visual skewering of a traumatizing parent. It can be created by constant parental neglect and rejection.

iii.   Self-abandonment: the fear and toxic shame that comes with the abandonment depression. It puts you in a state of total helplessness and hopelessness that you felt as a child.

iv.   A vicious inner critic

v.   Social anxiety

Other important facts about CPTSD

1. CPTSD is imbibed.

It isn't something you're born with. A person living with PTSD has an inability to complete many important developmental tasks. This means you can live free from CPTSD since it isn't in your DNA. You can unlearn it because you learned it.

2. Reparenting by committee.

Another good thing about CPTSD is that it has important self-help and relational components. Relational components mean you can have help from people around you. This could be family, friends, teachers, authors, therapists, teachers, partners, or therapeutic groups.

3. Other ways of finding help

In some cases where survivors of CPTSD were deeply betrayed by families – especially their parents – some of these survivors don't get over it easily. This usually happens because it takes a lot of work to trust someone else so that relational healing can begin. The other ways to find help in cases like these would be through pets, books, and online therapeutic websites.

4. Other signs of CPTSD

- The abject feeling of loneliness and abandonment
- Fragile self-esteem
- Developmental arrests
- Relationship difficulties
- Radical mood vacillation
- Suicidal ideation
- Oversensitivity to stressful situations
- Dissociation via distracting activities or mental processes

5. The 4Fs

Fight response is triggered when a person suddenly responds aggressively to something threatening. A flight response is triggered when a person responds to a perceived threat by fleeing or symbolically by launching into hyperactivity. A freeze response is triggered when a person, realizing resistance is futile, gives up or numbs out into dissociation and/or collapses as if accepting the inevitability of being hurt. A fawn response is triggered when a person responds to a threat by trying to be pleasing or helpful in order to appease and forestall an attacker.

Key takeaways from this chapter

- Contempt is a toxic cocktail of verbal and emotional abuse, a deadly amalgam of denigration, rage, and disgust
- Rage creates fear and disgust creates shame in a child. Eventually, it makes the child stops seeking help or connection from anyone.
- Trauma occurs when an attack or abandonment triggers a fight/flight response so that the person can't step out of the ambience of it even when the threat is over.
- Traumatized children often over-gravitate to one of the 4Fs to survive. After a while, the four modes become elaborated into entrenched defensive structures that are similar to narcissistic (fight), obsessive/compulsive (flight), dissociative (freeze), or codependent (fawn) defenses.

- When contempt replaces the milk of human kindness at an early age, the child feels humiliated and overwhelmed. Eventually, the child becomes defective and fatally flawed and believes that they deserve it.
- Sibling rivalry is further reinforced in dysfunctional families by the fact that all the children are substituting for minimal nurturance and are therefore without resources to give each other. Competition for the little affection provided by their parents turns them into fierce rivals.

Lessons

Traumatizing abuse and abandonment from our childhood damage us. There's an epidemic of traumatizing families all around the world. This can be in a verbal, physical, emotional, spiritual or even sexual form.

When abuse or neglect becomes severe without caution or help, it will lead to CPTSD. As it deepens, CPTSD worsens in a child. Some children who suffered CPTSD as a child grew up with it.

It's possible to get healed. This book is a blueprint for that.

Goals

- To recognize that CPTSD can come from growing up in an abusive or neglectful family.
- To take steps towards freedom from years of traumatizing abuse.

Action plans

- Take the necessary steps towards healing, even if it involves reflecting on certain unpleasant experiences.
- Accept that some point in this journey will deeply resonate with you and produce a mélange of feelings.
- Do not block those emotions; process them

Questions

1. What's the difference between active and passive suicidality? When do you need to get help?

2. What can you learn or gain when you're in a suicidal reverie?

3. Is CPTSD the same as a panic disorder? What's the difference if any?

4. What is the effect of contempt on a child?

5. Can emotional neglect in a child lead to a life of CPTSD? Can you describe how it happens?

6. Looking at all that has been discussed in this chapter, why is it important for a child to have a safe, trauma-free, happy, and emotionally healthy childhood?

7. What are the good sides and bad sides to growing up and living with the 4Fs?

CHAPTER 2: LEVELS OF RECOVERING

Summary

One thing that makes CPTSD complex is that it's a combination of many wounds over the years and it isn't from a singular event. This is what makes a one-dimensional solution almost impossible.

If you grew up with abusive and abandoning parents, you'll grow up injured and abandoned in a cognitive, relational, physical, emotional, and spiritual manner.

Effective recovery is releasing or unwinding your innate natural potential that is yet to be unrealized due to the trauma you went through as a child.

A tragic developmental arrest that many survivors experience is that they easily lose their willpower and self-motivation. This happens because many dysfunctional parents react destructively to their child's budding sense of initiative. If this continues during the survivor's childhood, the survivor may feel lost and purposeless in life.

Survivors learn to develop the imposter syndrome which is a result of confidence without self-esteem. It makes the individual confident in their abilities even though they have no self-esteem.

Cognitive healing and recovery make your brain user-friendly by identifying and removing the destructive thought and thinking that shaped you right from childhood.

Steps to help you carry out cognitive therapy

- You need someone to guide you (therapist)
- Identify the troubling thought or belief and what triggers it
- Acknowledge your emotions and belief about the troubling thought
- Spot the negative thinking about it
- Begin to change your thoughts about it

Early abuse and abandonment make children merge their identities with their superego. This way, the child gains acceptance because she knows how to please her caretakers while working on a way to win her parents over. This eventually leads to perfectionism. Perfectionism leads to self-criticism.

Ego is the same as who you are or your identity (according to psychology) which means it's not bad as we have always believed it is. Abusive parents hinder its growth which limits self-compassion and self-protection.

Mindfulness is taking out time without distractions so you can be aware of your thoughts and feelings and decide how you'll respond to them. According to John Kabat-Zinn, it's a way to befriend ourselves and our experiences.

Emotional intelligence is the ability to properly identify and manage our feelings so we respond accurately to the feeling of others. Our emotions can't be overlooked because according to Carl Jung, it is the chief source of becoming conscious.

Grieving helps us reconnect with our full complement of feelings.

Food helps us self-soothe. When a child starves of love, he makes food his love object.

Key takeaways of this chapter

- Healing from Complex PTSD is complex. There's nothing simple about it.
- Factors affecting your developmental arrest include your 4F type, your childhood abuse/neglect pattern, your innate nature, and the recovery work you already began.
- As a survivor, your ability to invoke willpower is linked to your ability to healthily express your anger.
- Cognitive healing repairs the damage CPTSD has on your beliefs and thoughts about yourself. It helps you upgrade the kind of story you tell yourself about the pain you feel.
- As important as cognitive tools are, they can't deal with all the wounds from the trauma and abuse you've experienced. (I'm sorry if you thought otherwise).
- Everyone needs a healthy ego.
- When you're continuously intimidated and shamed as a child, you'll lack sympathy and compassion for yourself and you'll be unable to stand up for yourself.
- Mindfulness brings together your instinct of self-compassion as well as your capacity for self-observation
- Grieving is the key process for reconnecting with our repressed emotional intelligence.

Lessons

- Don't be quick to settle for simplistic approaches to solve CPTSD. It will leave you disappointed and make you settle into toxic shame when you don't gain the results that it claims to provide.
- To recover, from the prison of your childhood, you have to learn how to support yourself which means you fill in the gaps from your childhood by providing yourself with the developmental needs on each level that is relevant to your experience of childhood trauma.
- Getting help from teachers, therapists, friends, and writers who have more wisdom and knowledge on cognitive healing is great.
- The more you identify the damage done by your parents, the more you can rectify it.

- You have to practice mindfulness to groom self-compassion and reshape your thoughts.
- If you hold on to a particular feeling longer than necessary, you'll appear to be unnatural and phony. It would seem like laughing at a joke after everyone has forgotten about the joke.
- Emotional abuse and neglect scare us out of our own emotions while making us scared of other people's feelings.
- When our emotional intelligence is restricted, we often do not know what we want and consequently struggle mightily with the smallest of decisions.
- Grieving restores our crucial, developmentally arrested capacity to verbally ventilate. Verbal ventilation is speaking from your feelings in a way that releases and resolves your emotional distress.
- Good enough parenting entails parents providing their children with love and support consistently that it grows their self-esteem and capacity for intimacy.
- The cultivation of gratitude requires a balanced perspective. You need to see and appreciate the good in life without giving up your ability to discern what is negative and unacceptable in the present.

Goals

- To gain insight and learn from the keychain of perspectives and techniques that will lead to freedom from the prison of your childhood.
- To practice cognitive healing.
- To let yourself have epiphanies about what is at the core of your suffering.
- To have a positive change of mind towards yourself.
- To gain a healthy ego.
- To gain emotional emancipation
- To improve my self-esteem
- To understand good parenting
- To gain somatic repair
- To gain dietary help

Action plans

- To look into areas of development without listening to the voice of restraint or resentment when you're trying to nurture yourself
- To see that you're free to develop inner peace and a great supportive relationship with yourself.
- Get psychoeducation about CPTSD
- To practice mindfulness
- To stop any attempt at disallowing negative emotions

- To practice verbal ventilation
- To cultivate gratitude
- To practice stretching, yoga, massage, meditation, and other relaxation techniques

Questions

1. Why is cognitive healing important?
2. What steps can you take to aid cognitive healing?
3. Can a sense of belonging heal years of trauma and abuse? Explain the reason for your answer.
4. How can grieving and verbal ventilation help you heal?
5. What signs of body-harming reactions to CPTSD stress have you experienced?
6. What can you do to gain somatic repair?
7. What leads to food addictions and how can it be corrected?

CHAPTER 3: IMPROVING RELATIONSHIPS

Summary

Some amazing ways to heal human connections, especially when it comes to betrayals, involve dogs, cats, nature, music, and arts. According to Heather L. Stuckey et al in the journal paper "The Connection Between Art, Healing, and Public Health," music engagement, visual art therapy, movement-based creative expression, and expressive writing are also other forms of therapies.

CPTSD has been seen as an attachment disorder because the child grew up without a safe adult to healthily bond with.

When the developmental need to practice healthy relating with a caretaker is unmet, survivors typically struggle to find and maintain healthy, supportive relationships in their adult lives.

When a child grows up without a reliable source of love, support, and protection, the child grows up into a great deal of unease and naturally becomes reluctant to seek support from anyone.

Signs of social anxiety

- Not trusting people
- Not expecting people to be there for you
- You're scared of needing something from others
- You don't like socializing because you feel awkward within but you look calm on the outside
- You fear that people would see how wretched and pitiful you are on the inside.

Sobbing and crying is a way to release pent-up emotions and allow yourself to be free.

Groups can be more helpful than individuals when it comes to healing from shame.

Co-counseling is another source of relational healing.

Intimacy with people isn't reason enough to have everything that you want. A healthy relationship involves disagreement, disaffection, and disappointments.

Re-parenting helps to address the many developmentally arrested needs of the traumatized child we were.

The Tao of relational recovery involves balancing healthy independence with a healthy dependence on others.

Key takeaways of this chapter

- Dogs and cats are good for children because according to Carl Rogers, they are the 'unconditional positive regard' they need to thrive. Music nature and arts can also help to attain healing.

- CPTSD has emotional neglect at its core.
- Attachment disorder or CPTSD leads to a lack of relational skills that create intimacy. This leads to social unease or anxiety.
- In some extreme cases, social anxiety can lead to social phobia, especially during prolonged flashbacks.
- Learn to cry; you'll find out that you feel okay afterward.
- Toxic shame can't be healed without relational help.
- Feeling compassion for someone who has suffered similarly to us sometimes naturally expands into feeling the same for ourselves.
- Insufficient self-compassion is the worst developmental arrest while restored self-compassion is the key to gaining effective recovery.
- If your parents are deeply toxic, their voice or a word from them can lead to an intense emotional flashback.
- The hallmark of successful couples is their ability to handle feelings of anger and hurt in a constructive and civil way.
- Self-compassion comes easy when a child's mothering needs are met. Self-protection comes easy when a child's fathering needs are met.
- Self-mothering helps you to see that you're lovable and deserve to be loved.
- The time machine rescue operation is a way to ward off an overwhelming sense of helplessness that often accompanies emotional flashbacks.
- The attainment of a safe supportive relationship with others helps you become more self-supportive.

Lessons

- Relational healing can come from non-human sources such as dogs, cats, nature, music, and art.
- When a child goes through attachment disorder, intimacy becomes difficult for the survivors when they are adults.
- Self-sufficiency is a survival strategy for children who grew up with abusive parents.
- Extensive childhood abuse installs a powerful people-are-dangerous program into survivors.
- Surrender yourself to weeping. It's a way to release yourself.
- There's more vulnerability in a group than in individual work.
- As self-compassion increases, toxic shame decreases.
- No one would accept you for yourself if you're abusively angry or contemptuous.
- Intimacy isn't unconditional love.
- We need self-compassion to recover but the foundation of self-compassion is self-protection.
- Safe human help always enhances recovery.
- The more self-supportive we become, the more we attract supportive others.

Goals

- To learn to trust others and improve relationships
- To learn to be vulnerable
- To build self-compassion
- To find healing
- To become an unshakeable source of compassion and protection for yourself
- Re-mothering and re-fathering yourself
- To learn re-parenting by committee

Action plans

- To get a pet
- To find music or art or nature that you can connect with
- Allow yourself to weep and wail
- To practice self-compassion for yourself and others
- To believe and see that you're lovable and deserve to be loved. Increase your self-compassion and unconditional positive regard. Refuse to indulge in self-hatred and self-abandonment. Don't punish yourself. Practice patience and self-encouragement with yourself. Reject self-judgment and self-rejection. Create a place in your heart where you're always welcome. Use healing words and affirmations instead of critical messages.
- Self-fathering heals you from the wounds of being helpless to protect yourself from parental abuse or abuse from figures of authority. It works to build assertiveness and self-protection, confront abuse, and stand up for a child's rights.
- To use time machine rescue operations to heal by thinking of going back in time and what you'll do differently.

Questions

1. Have you ever felt a connection to music or art or any other thing that you always have to go back to it when you don't feel good about yourself?
2. Can you identify situations or events that made you nervous?
3. Do you find it difficult to trust others or seek help from others? Can you identify the reason behind this?
4. Do you believe weeping can provide relief when you feel overwhelmed? Explain the reason for your answer.
5. 5. Why is getting relational help important?
6. Do you believe therapeutic relational experiences can help you groom self-compassion?
7. What is the key to enhancing recovery?

CHAPTER 4: THE PROGRESSION OF RECOVERING

Summary

Signs to show that you're recovering

- The reduction of emotional flashbacks
- You're more friendly to yourself and you reduce the way you criticize yourself
- You're less of a perfectionist
- You can easily relax
- You don't easily overreact from a triggered position or intense emotion
- You use the 4Fs in a healthy way
- You're more balanced
- You can relax when you're in the company of the people you feel safe with
- You want to take care of yourself
- You're more optimistic hopeful and certain that you're recovering

To a large extent, recovery is progressive. If the recovery is effective, you'll notice progress in one or two areas at a time. To expect progress at all times and all levels is to live in denial.

The stages of recovery begin from a cognitive level. Here's how to identify the stages of recovery

- Practice mindfulness and gain psychoeducation
- Shrink the critic
- Grieve your childhood
- Face the abandonment depression you feel
- Practice critic shrinking

It's about progress, not perfection.

With self-acceptance, self-compassion, and patience, survival mode and regressions are easier to handle.

Early in your recovery stage, it's normal to dismiss your progress because you expect 100% progress in all areas at once.

Areas survivors fail to notice their progress

- Less intense launching into the 4Fs response
- You're more resistant to your inner critic
- You practice mindfulness more than before especially when your critic is awakened or when the flashbacks come
- You feel good about yourself more

- You don't overeat or self-medicate. Sometimes you find yourself doing this but it's reduced.
- You're better at relating with others
- The intensity and painfulness attached to the flashbacks are reduced.

Taking note of your progress encourages you to keep at it.

Encourage yourself to face the pains that come from intense emotions and flashbacks by seeing them as therapeutic flashbacks. It's like going through the pain of surgery so you can get better afterward.

Optimal stress is the balanced, moderate amount of stress necessary to grow the new neurons and neuronal connections that correlate with keeping the brain healthy.

Emotional intelligence is a foundational ingredient of relational intelligence.

The survivor who pursues long-term development on his journey to recovery generally achieves greater overall evolution than the average citizen.

Contagious joy is the wonderful triggered into vicariously sharing someone else's authentic delight.

Key takeaways of this chapter

- With enough practice, you'll be able to manage situations that trigger flashbacks.
- Recovery begins on a cognitive level where psychoeducation and mindfulness help us to see that we have CPTSD.
- Sometimes the process of recovery can feel so demanding and complex that you feel stuck in inertia for a long time.
- Your emotions can feel topsy-turvy. Recovery means you're learning how to handle it.
- Your journey to progress moves from surviving to thriving. When you're on top of it and progressing, you can easily point out the signs of progress. When you're at the extreme of thriving, you're surviving. Everything you did to progress and thrive feels too difficult and you want to give up.
- Regressions are how our psyche tells us to address important developmental arrests.
- If you can't identify your progress even when you're progressing, you'll give up.
- Viewing everything in black and white (thinking progress is either 100% or there's no progress) will not help recovery.
- Recovery and progression are lifelong processes. They never truly end.
- Feelings of love, appreciation, and gratitude are naturally enhanced when we reciprocally show ourselves whether we are afraid or confident, loving or alienated, proud or embarrassed.

Lessons

- The reduction of flashbacks both in occurrences and intensity will be a result of your proficiency at managing the trigger.
- Recovery is progressive in nature. It is a culmination of many right little steps.
- Recovery is complex.
- Progress is what you're aiming for not perfection.
- When you're in survival mode, everything feels pretty much awful. Flashback can morph into extended regressions.
- Pay attention to yourself so you notice your recovery and progress.
- Your inner critic can't see any sign of progress. Don't identify with it.
- You need bravery to find your real voice.

Goals

- To measure the progress in recovery
- Giving up salvation fantasy
- To practice self-compassion
- To stop trying to fix everything at once
- To stop criticizing yourself
- To find your balance when you're in survival mode
- To learn optimal stress
- To stay joyful

Action plans

1. To reduce emotional flashbacks

Ask yourself:

- What always happens just before I feel those intense emotions? What can I do about it?
- If it is someone I love that feels these intense emotions, what would I tell her to help her?

2. Giving up salvation fantasy
- Remember that recovery is almost the same as growing up as a child. While growing and learning to walk, you fall and get back up.
- It's almost impossible to be totally flashback-free

3. Re-parenting yourself
- Remember to tell yourself it's normal to have these flashbacks once in a while.
- Be kind to yourself. Having a flashback doesn't make you evil. It means you're only human.

4. Keep progressing
- Acknowledge that you have CPTSD
- Practice mindfulness
- Grieve over all the intense emotions you feel. Grieve over how you felt as a child.
- Be patient with yourself. Focus on progression, not perfection
- Feelings of fear, shame and guilt are sometimes signs that we've done the right thing. They are emotional flashbacks to how we were traumatized.

5. To get through survival
- You need to realize that you've come a long way. That you know you have CPTSD is progress in itself.

6. Silencing your inner critic
- Try journaling. Keep a record of your daily activities, especially about times you felt intense emotions. Make sure you note how much it has reduced. Take note of the reduction and recurrence of shame, fear, and depression. Compare it and see how much you're improving.
- Don't see life in white and black; that's what makes you say I'm not recovering at all because you want to see a perfect recovery.
- Accept recovery as lifelong progress.
- The path of recovery is filled with temporary setbacks.

7. Learning optimal stress
- Read self-help books
- Attend self-improvement workshops
- Journaling

Questions

1. Your inner critic tells you that you're not recovering or progressing. What would you look out for to know you're progressing?
2. Someone you know is recovering from CPTSD and you can see the signs. He believes he will no longer have intense emotional flashbacks. Is this true? What's the reason for your answer?
3. Why are self-medication and self-soothing not the way forward?
4. What's the way forward when it comes to attaining deeper intimacy?
5. Why is introspective development important?
6. Why is porn addiction not healthy for survivors?

PART II: THE FINE POINT OF RECOVERING

CHAPTER 5: WHAT IF I WAS NEVER HIT?

Summary

Denial about the traumatic effects of childhood abandonment can seriously hamper your ability to recover.

Verbal abuse is more damaging than physical abuse.

Fear and shame teach a child to stop asking for attention and to stop seeking to express himself in ways that draw attention. Eventually, the child stops seeking any form of connection.

Unrelenting criticism from parental scorn and rage changes the structure of a child's brain as the child keeps repeating them to himself. This leads to a thick neural pathway of self-hate and self-disgust. This will also lead to a crippling state of self-attack and self-abandonment. The child eventually is unable to support himself or be on his own side.

You will constantly find yourself in denial when you minimize the damage caused by extensive emotional neglect.

Traumatic emotional neglect occurs when a child doesn't have a single caretaker to turn to in time of need or danger. CPTSD sets in when there is no alternative adult to turn to for comfort and protection.

Failure to thrive is not an all-or-none phenomenon but rather a continuum that stretches from the abandonment depression to death.

When the survivor has no understanding of the effects of trauma or no memory of being traumatized, addictions are often understandable, misplaced attempts to regulate painful emotional flashbacks.

When children experience long periods of being powerless to obtain the needed connection with a parent, they become increasingly anxious, upset, and depressed.

When there's no emotional and relational intelligence due to abandoning parents, children don't know that a relationship with a healthy person can be comforting and enriching.

While dealing with denial, allow yourself to cry those bitter-sweet tears. It's bitter because you realize that abandonment was more devastating than you realize, and sweet because it validates the truth of the recollection and put the blame where it truly belongs. The tears will keep switching from bitter to sweet and sweet to bitter.

Deep level recovery is often reflected in a narrative that highlights the role of emotional neglect in describing what one has suffered and what one continues to deal with.

Key takeaways of this chapter

- In childhood, ongoing emotional neglect creates overwhelming feelings of fear, shame, and emptiness.
- Words that are filled with contempt infuse the child and make a child full of fear and toxic shame.
- A childhood rife with emotional and verbal abuse forces the child to identify with the critic so strongly that it becomes her identity.
- Growing up emotionally neglected is like nearly dying of thirst outside the fenced-off fountain of a parent's warmth and interest.
- Without the presence of a nurturing caretaker, love starvation increases and sometimes moves the child into a failure to thrive syndrome.
- Substance and process addictions can be seen as misguided attempts to distract from the inner pain.
- Once a child's dominant experience of herself is filled with unmanageable emotional pain, she begins to self-medicate, act out (gets aggressive towards others), or act in (aggressive against herself) to get distracted from it.
- Lack of emotional intelligence and relational intelligence leads to an inability to open up to and benefit from the love and care of others.
- Understanding how derelict your parents were in their duty to protect you is a master key to your recovery.

Lessons

- Recovery depends on realizing that fear, shame, and depression are a result of a loveless childhood.
- The assault from words destroys our self-esteem, replacing it with a toxic inner critic that incessantly judges us as defective.
- Emotional neglect makes children feel worthless, unlovable, and excruciatingly empty.
- In CPTSD-engendering families, the absence of care and concern is extreme; a caretaker is rarely or never available for support, comfort, or protection. Without the presence of a caretaker in a child's life, the child becomes an increasingly nightmarish amalgam of fear, shame, and depression.
- Emotional abandonment is healed by real intimacy.

Goals

- To confront denial
- To disidentify from the critic
- To get over emotional neglect

- To grieve
- To reconstruct your childhood
- To learn how to be vulnerable
- To practice self-compassion

Action plans

1. Practicing de-minimization
   - See that this is a lifetime process.
   - Ask yourself what could have been worse than your childhood trauma. What scenarios would you think of as worse than how you grew up? You can search online to find such stories.

2. Liberation from the critic
   - Forgive yourself for going back into self-blame constantly
   - Remember that progress is a back and forth process
   - Don't give up the fight
   - Re-mother yourself by trying to be self-compassionate.

3. Getting over emotional neglect
   - Acknowledge how you feel about your childhood emotional neglect. Don't stay in denial.

4. Getting over substance addiction
   - Grieve. Don't block the pain you feel.

5. Learning to be vulnerable
   - There must be someone or a group of people you're willing to speak up and share how you feel.
   - According to Criss Jami, to share your weakness is to make yourself vulnerable; to make yourself vulnerable is to show your strength.
   - Allow yourself to cry.

Questions

1. What's the downside to emotional neglect? What is the effect on a child?
2. Is there a link between emotional hunger and substance abuse? What's the link (if any)?
3. What are the things that give rise to the inner critic?
4. What is the role of the media in a child living with CPTSD?
5. What are the signs to show that you grew up in a CPTSD engendering family?

CHAPTER 6: WHAT IS MY TRAUMA TYPE

Summary

People who are repetitively traumatized in childhood often learn to survive by using one or two of their 4F responses.

Positive attributes of the 4Fs

Fight	Flight	Freeze	Fawn
Assertiveness	Disengagement	Acute awareness	Love and science
Boundaries	Healthy retreat	Mindfulness	Compromise
Courage	Industrious	Poised Readiness	Listening
Moxie	Know-how	Peace	Fairness
Leadership	Perseverance	presence	Peacemaking

Negative attributes of the 4F defenses

Fight	Flight	Freeze	Fawn
Narcissistic	Obsessive/Compulsive disorder	Codependent	
Explosive	Panicky	Contracting	Obsequious
Controlling	Rushing or worrying	Hiding	Servitude
(Enslaving)	(Outrunning pain)	(Camouflaging)	(Groveling)
Entitlement	Driven-ness	Isolation	Loss of self
Type-A	Adrenaline junkie	Couch potato	People pleaser
Bully	Busyholic	Space case	Doormat
Autocrat	Micromanager	Hermit	Slave
Demands	Compelled by	Achievement	Social
Perfection	Perfectionism	Phobic	Perfectionism
Sociopath	Mood disorder (bipolar) schizophrenic	D.V. victim	
Conduct disorder	ADHD	ADD	Parentified child

4Fs distortions of attachment and safety instincts

Fight	Flight	Freeze	Fawn
Control	Perfect	No way	Merge
To connect	To connect	I'll connect	To connect
Rage	Perfect	Hide	Grovel
To be safe	To be safe	To be safe	To be safe

The fight-fawn hybrid combines narcissism and codependence. This is in contrast with the fawn-fight hybrid. The former hardly take the blame for any real responsibility for contributing to an interpersonal problem.

The flight-freeze hybrid is the least relational and most schizoid. They are usually misdiagnosed as Asperger's syndrome. They are more prone to becoming porn addicts and when in flight mode they obsessively surf the net for phantom partners and engage in compulsive masturbation. When in freeze mode they drift into a right-brain sexual fantasy world if porn is unavailable.

The fight-freeze hybrid rarely seeks recovery on its own. Sometimes a threat can be the only thing that drags them to therapy. They are a passive narcissist; they want things to go their way and they aren't interested in any human interaction.

Key takeaways of this chapter

- People with good enough parenting in childhood arrive in adulthood with a healthy and flexible response to danger. In face of real danger, they have access to all their 4F choices.
- Excessive reliance on a fight, flight, freeze, or fawn response is the traumatized child's unconscious attempt to cope with constant danger and a strategy to strengthen the illusion that her parents really care about her.
- A survivor avoids vulnerable relating because his past makes him believe that he will be attacked or abandoned as he was in childhood.
- Fight types are unconsciously driven by the belief that power and control can create safety, assuage abandonment, and secure love.

What to know about fight types

1. Those who are more likely to become fight type/narcissistic defense
   - Spoiled children
   - Children who have insufficient limits
   - Children who imitate the bullying of a narcissistic parent
   - Children who easily get into fights
   - Older siblings who over-power their younger siblings
2. They respond to their feelings of abandonment with anger. They infuse contempt, rage, and disgust to intimidate and shame others into mirroring them, the very person they want to avoid.
3. Some fight types are sociopathic. They depend on scapegoats for the dumping of their vitriol.
4. There are rageaholic narcissists. They are infamous for using others as a dumping ground for their anger.
5. There are charming narcissists. They make you feel like they are interested in you and then shift all the focus to themselves by monologing. You are already a captive and wouldn't be easily released.

6. Fight types need to see how their condescending moral high ground
7. They must renounce the illusion of their perfection and habit of projecting perfectionistic inner critic processes onto others.
8. They need to take self-initiated timeouts whenever they are triggered and feel overcritical.

What to know about the flight type and the obsessive-compulsive defense

1. They believe perfection makes them lovable.
2. They flee the inner pain of abandonment with the symbolic flight of constant busyness.
3. When she isn't in an obsessive-compulsive state, she's worrying and planning about doing. Obsessive-compulsive is a left-brain dissociation which is the use of constant thinking to distract yourself from underlying abandonment pain.
4. They are prone to becoming addicted to their own adrenaline.
5. They are over-analytical

What to know about the freeze type/dissociative defense

1. It triggers a survivor into hiding, isolating, and avoiding human contact.
2. They have a deep-seated consciousness that people and danger are synonymous.
3. They take refuge in solitude
4. Children who are the scapegoats, the abandoned, or the lost are forced to habituate the freeze response.
5. They have a right-brain dissociation. This allows them to disconnect from experiencing abandonment pain or risky social interactions because it can trigger feelings of being traumatized.
6. They enjoy long bouts of sleep, daydreaming, wishing, internet surfing, and living virtually.
7. They know how to switch their inner channel when one experience becomes uncomfortable.
8. They are content with themselves and they can self-medicate.

What to know about the fawn type/ codependent defense

1. They merge with the needs and demands of others.
2. They are confidants to their parents, substitute spouse or coach, or housekeeper
3. They are the most developmentally arrested in their healthy sense of self.

Lessons

- Over time, a habitual 4F dense serves to distract us from the nagging voice of the critic and the painful feelings that underlie it.

- The 4Fs are commonly ambivalent about real intimacy because closeness often triggers us into painful emotional flashbacks.
- Fight types benefit from learning to redirect their rage towards the awful childhood circumstances that caused them to adopt such an intimacy-destroying defense. As the fight type becomes more conscious of his abandonment feelings, he can learn to release his fear and shame with tears.
- Without practicing consideration for others and without reciprocity and dialogicality, the intimacy you crave will allude you.

Goals

- To improve the possibility of intimacy
- To recover from a polarized fight mode
- To recover from a polarized flight response
- To have easy and appropriate access to all of the 4fs

Action plans

1. To deal with abandonment feelings
   - Release your fear and shame with tears. Don't keep the anger within.
   - Take timeouts when your original abandonment feelings surface

2. How to recover from a fight position
   - Learn the empathy of a fawn position
   - Try to listen properly and interact with the person you're interacting with.
   - Develop mindfulness about the needs, rights, and feelings of those with whom you'll love to have real intimacy. Spend time understanding them.

3. How to recover from a polarized flight response
   - Introspect out loud.
   - Practice self-compassionate crying. It shrinks the obsessive perseverations of the critic.
   - Stay neutral. Sometimes deliberately decide not to do anything. You can spend this time meditating even if it's for three or five minutes before you begin your day. Start a chair meditation by closing your eyes, and gently asking your body to relax. Take deep breaths and feel your muscles relax. 'Ask yourself what's the most important priority?' As you 'What hurt am I running from' or 'Can I open my heart to the idea and image of soothing myself in my pain?'
   - Get self-help books, CDs, or classes to help you relax. You can use music, drawing, or art to do the same.

- Tell yourself: 'don't just do something, stand there.' This makes you become centered and helps you re-prioritize.
4. How to recover from a polarized freeze response
    - Get therapy in place of isolation. Build a therapeutic relationship
    - Get a pet.
5. How to recover from a polarized fawn response
    Get psychoeducation
    Be more expressive by broadening your verbal and emotional self-expression. Speak out.

Questions

1. When faced with a relationship, how do you react? As a fight, flight, freeze or fawn?
2. Think about a past relationship you had or almost had. With the knowledge you have now about CPTSD, what would you have done differently?
3. Go through all the 4Fs and determine where you fall.

3b. Do the same for your siblings.

CHAPTER 7: RECOVERING FROM TRAUMA-BASED CODEPENDENCY

Summary

The fawn response makes a survivor apologize for everything and anything. As a survivor, you're addicted to apologizing. You learn very early to delete 'no' from your dictionary and never develop the language of healthy assertiveness.

Qualities of the fawn type survivor

- Servitude, ingratiation, and obsequiousness are important survival strategies for the fawn type of survivor.
- She forfeits the needs that might inconvenience her parents and obliterates preferences and opinions that might annoy them.
- She surrenders her opinions and boundaries to satisfy her parents
- She seeks safety and acceptance in a relationship through listening and eliciting.

Trauma-induced codependency is a syndrome of self-abandonment and self-abnegation.

Codependency is a fear-based inability to express rights, needs, and boundaries in a relationship. It is a disorder of assertiveness, characterized by a dormant fight response and a susceptibility to being exploited, abused, and/or neglected.

Fawn-freeze type

- The scapegoat
- Most likely to be victimized as an adult
- Most likely to be subjected to domestic violence
- Easily blames herself
- They make little effort at recovery
- They live in learned selflessness

Fawn-flight: Super Nurse

- The busyholic parent, nurse, or administrative assistant who works from dusk till dawn until bedtime providing for the needs of the household, hospital or company. She takes care of everyone but rarely without thinking of himself.
- She's a Mother Theresa who escapes the pain of her self-abandonment by seeing herself as the perfect selfless caregiver. She distances herself from her pain by obsessive-compulsively rushing from one person to another.
- She can become an OCD-like clean-holic.
- She can easily overburden others with advice.

Fawn-fight: Smother Mother

- She can be aggressive in her attempt to help others
- She can alienate others by persistently pressuring them to take her advice.
- She over-focuses on others because she had a servant role as a child.
- In flashback, she can deteriorate into manipulative or even coercive care-taking by loving people until they become who she wants them to be.
- She is relational and most susceptible to love and sex addiction.

Pretense is a sign of dysfunctional emotional matching. It shows as

- Being amused at destructive sarcasm
- Feigning love when someone is punishing you
- Acting forgiving when someone is repetitively hurtful

Key takeaways of this chapter

- Sudden anxiety responses to apparently innocuous circumstances are often emotional flashbacks to earlier traumatic events.
- The loss of self for a fawn survivor happens early, even before she learns how to talk properly
- Extreme emotional abandonment creates the fawn kind of codependency. Once a child realizes that being useful and not requiring anything for herself gets her some positive attention from her parents, codependency begins to grow.
- Safety is what directs a fawn survivor. She believes it is safer to listen than to talk, to agree than to dissent, to offer care than to ask for help, to elicit the other than to express yourself, and to leave choices to the other person than to express preferences.
- When triggered into a panicky sense of abandonment, the smothering mother feels desperate for love and can vacillate dramatically between clawing for it or flattering groveling for it.
- Recovering from a polarized fawn response begins with understanding that the codependence of the survivor comes from continuously being attacked and shamed as selfish. Understand that fear of being attacked for lapses in ingratiation is what has made you forfeit your boundaries.
- It is a great accomplishment to significantly reduce verbal matching and a more powerful achievement to reduce inauthentic emotional mirroring.

Lessons

- Sometimes a current event can have only the vaguest resemblance to a past traumatic situation, and this can be enough to trigger the psyche's hard-wiring for a fight, flight, freeze, or fawn response.
- Fawns work well with narcissists because they enable their monologing.

- When we emotionally remember how overpowered we were as children, we can begin to realize that it was because we were too small and powerless to assert ourselves. As adults, we are much more powerful and we can decide to be assertive.
- Grieving unlocks healthy anger about a life lived with such a diminished sense of self.
- Recovering requires us to become increasingly mindful of our automatic matching and mirroring behaviors. This helps to decrease the habit of reflexively agreeing with everything that anyone says.

Goals

- To understand your fawn type
- To get unhooked from the fawn-freeze scapegoat
- To step out of the fawn-fight mentality.
- To deconstruct codependence
- To gain assertiveness
- To understand disapproval is okay.

Action plans

1. To get unhooked from the fawn-freeze
   - Understand how your childhood abuse is the foundation of your current abuse
   - Learn to speak up. Begin by journaling and meditating about it.

2. To step away from the super nurse mentality
   - Caring isn't all about fixing
   - Understand that we are all human so we can be imperfect
   - Don't repeat your advice after saying it once.

3. To stop being the smother mother
   - Everyone has a right to be weak
   - It's not your place to fix everyone
   - Your advice is simply your advice. Everyone has the option to take it or leave it.
   - You don't have to love people to death. If you really love people, learn to leave them alone and let them be free.

4. Deconstructing codependence
   - Cry about the loss and pain of being so long without healthy self-interest and self-protection.
   - Stop focusing on what other people want and stop trying to read them. Stay with your own experiences.
   - Reclaiming assertiveness

- Think of a situation in your past where you were unfairly treated. Stay present to your fear so you can see how your fears trigger you into fawning and act assertively. Try to do it as much as you can but not too much.

Questions

1. How can you care for someone without trying to fix the person's problems?
2. How can you be free from codependence?
3. Why is empathy important for fawns?

CHAPTER 8: MANAGING EMOTIONAL FLASHBACKS

Summary

Emotional flashbacks are intensely disturbing regressions (amygdala hijackings) to the overwhelming feeling-states of your childhood abandonment.

Common experiences to help you identify an emotional flashback

- You feel little, fragile, and helpless
- Everything feels too hard
- Life is too scary
- Being seen feels excruciatingly vulnerable
- Your battery seems to be dead
- In the worst flashback an apocalypse feels like it will imminently be upon you.
- When you're trapped in a flashback, you're relieving the worst emotional times of your childhood.
- Everything feels overwhelming and confusing

13 steps for managing emotional flashbacks

1. Say to yourself: I'm having a flashback
2. Remind yourself: 'I feel afraid but I'm not in danger!'
3. Own your right/need to have boundaries.
4. Speak reassuringly to the inner child.
5. Deconstruct eternity thinking
6. Remind yourself that you're in an adult body
7. Ease back into your body by
    - Gently asking your body to relax
    - Breathing deeply and slowly
    - Slow down
    - Find a safe place
    - Feel the fear in your body without reacting to it
8. Resist the inner critic's drasticizing and catastrophizing.
    - Use thought-stopping to halt the critic's endless exaggerations of danger and its constant planning to control the uncontrollable
    - Use thought-substitution and thought correction to replace negative thinking
9. Allow yourself to grieve
10. Cultivate safe relationships and seek support
11. Learn to identify the triggers that lead to flashbacks
12. Figure out what you're flashing back to
13. Be patient with a slow recovery process

Resolving a flashback requires rebalancing significant changes in the brain and body that take time to subside. For instance, over-adrenalization sometimes morphs into the hangover of adrenalin exhaustion before the adrenal function can be rebalanced.

How to identify you're in a flashback

- An increase in the virulence of the inner or outer critic. There's an intensified self-criticism and/or judgment of others.
- Our emotional reactions are out of proportion to what triggered them. A minor upset feels like an emergency and a minor unfairness feels like a travesty of justice.
- You have a stronger urge to use a substance to alter your mood.
- You have hypochondriasizing ruminations about my health
- You neglect yourself due to the old pain of self-abandonment.

Key takeaways of this chapter

- Amygdala hijackings are intense reactions in the emotional memory part of the brain that override the rational brain. These reactions occur in the brains of people who have been triggered into a 4F so often that minor events can now trigger them into a panicky state.
- A trigger is an external or internal stimulus that activates us into an emotional flashback.
- The look can be an emotional trigger. It's a facial expression that typically accompanies contempt. It can work after a parent dies.
- While internal triggering is at its worst, small potato miscues and peccadilloes trigger us into full-blown emotional flashbacks. This leads to a polarized process of negative-noticing, an incessant preoccupation with defects and hazards.
- Flashbacks make us forget that our proven allies are in fact still reliable.
- A dream can trigger you into a flashback.
- See flashbacks as a communication from the child that you were.
- An unpredictable shift in your emotional weather is a typical CPTSD challenge.

Lessons

- When you're stuck in a flashback, fear, shame, and/or depression can dominate your experience.
- As intense as flashbacks may feel (due to the feelings and sensations from past memories), they can't hurt you now.
- When you're mindful of the triggers it allows you to avoid flashback-inducing people, situations, and behaviors.
- The worst thing about having been traumatized by The Look in childhood is that we can erroneously transfer and project our memory of it onto other people when we are triggered.

Goals

- To manage emotional flashbacks
- To keep progressing on the path of recovery

Action plans

1. To keep progressing
   - Post a copy of the 13 steps where you can see it first thing in the morning and the last thing at night. Read it to yourself first thing in the morning and the last thing at night.

2. To identify triggers
   - Identify the external triggers around you
   - Identify other common triggers as well. A look can be a trigger.

3. To choose healthy flashbacks management
   - Acknowledge that flashbacks are the real emergencies and injustices of our childhood
   - Understand and see it as a sign that you were traumatized
   - Choose self-care and self-compassion always

4. To stop self-medication
   - Don't overeat, especially when you're having a flashback
   - Don't indulge in mood-altering activities or substances

5. To help other children manage emotional flashbacks
   - Ask the child if she has felt that way before while explaining how you feel
   - Help her relax especially with a soft easy tone of voice to reassure her. Tell her she's safe with you so she can see that adults are interested in protecting her.
   - Guide her mind back to her body. Teach her to take slow breaths, to relax her muscles, to slow down to identify and encourage retreat to a safe place, and to draw, stretch, practice yoga or Tai Chi.
   - Encourage her to talk and use her words.
   - Encourage her to cry so she can grieve the death of feeling safe.
   - Help her build a memorized list of qualities, assets, successes, and resources to shrink the inner critic
   - Use cartoons, songs, and superheroes to help her identify her 4F type and its positive side
   - Let her know she has the right to have boundaries and the right to say no.
   - Teach her to identify and avoid dangerous people and places
   - Help her to see that she has a safe future

Questions

1. Why is it for you to post and read your 13 steps every day?
2. Why is it important to be mindful of what triggers you?
3. Why does the look continue even after the death of a parent?
4. What is more important and why? is it recognizing the moment of triggering or recognizing the trigger?
5. How can you help your young niece or neighbor's child manage emotional flashbacks?

CHAPTER 9: SHRINKING THE INNER CRITIC

Summary

When parents do not provide safe enough bonding and positive feedback, it makes the child flounder in anxiety and fear. Many children appear to be hard-wired to adapt to this endangering abandonment with perfectionism.

When perfectionism striving fails to win the acceptance of your parents, the inner critic becomes increasingly hostile and caustic. It festers into a virulent inner voice that increasingly manifests self-hate, self-disgust, and self-abandonment, blaming you for shortcomings that it imagines to be the cause of your parents' rejection.

Hypervigilance is a fixation on looking for danger that comes from excessive exposure to real danger. This is a result of the trauma you faced as a child.

14 common inner critic attacks

1. Perfectionism
2. All-or-none and black-and-white thinking
3. Self-hate, self-disgust, and toxic shame
4. Micromanagement/worrying/obsessing/looping/over-futurizing
5. Unfair/devaluing comparisons to others or to your perfect moments
6. Guilt
7. Shoulding
8. Overproductivity/workaholism/busy-holism
9. Harsh judgments on self and others or name-calling
10. Drasticizing or catastrophizing or hypochondriasizing
11. Negative focus
12. Time urgency
13. Disabling performance anxiety
14. Perseverating about being attacked

Perspective-substitution is a great strategy to correct your mindset. It is a tool that defeats or shrinks the inner critic as it helps you see the world from a broader perspective which is effective at changing your narrative from a negative one to a balanced and accurate focus of the observing ego.

Scientists have been able to prove the neuroplasticity of the brain. This means the brain can grow and change throughout our lifetime.

Key takeaways of this chapter
- A flashback-inducing critic is typically spawned in a danger-ridden childhood home.
- The cruel totalitarian inner critic is a key distinguishing feature of CPTSD.

- The inner critic is a process. It is an ever-developing process that co-opts our creativity and finds new and improved ways of imitating our parents' disparagement.
- Toxic shame is the emotional matrix of the abandonment depression. And it keeps us stuck in flashbacks. It is the emotional tone of the inner critic.
- Perfectionism is an instinctual defense for emotionally abandoned children because it saves the child from giving up until lack of success forces her to retreat into a dissociative freeze.
- A typical indication that the critic has mellowed into being functional is that it speaks to us in a kind and helpful voice.
- Without perspective substitution, no change is bound to happen. Our minds can't function in a vacuum. If you are dethroning the perspective you have from your inner critic, you must enthrone new and healthy perspectives.
- Gratitude is not a denial of all that happened or is happening to you. It helps you keep track of all the good things around you and with enough practice, you'll gravitate to gratitude without thinking about it.

Lessons

- The inner critic is the superego gone bad and in overdrive desperately trying to win your parents' approval.
- The inner critic triggers overwhelming emotional flashbacks.
- Parents who reject a child typically make the child believe his opinions and feelings are dangerous imperfections. In some cases, the impulse to speak triggers fear and shame.
- The critic is a constant hypervigilance that sees disaster hovering in the next moment.
- To shrink the critic, you need thousands of angry skirmishes with the critic. With growth and enough practice, the survivor's healthy ego can use willpower alone to disidentify from the critic.
- Thought substitution is another essential tool for empowering the work of stopping the critic.
- The most important thought of all is a switch in the perspective of our thinking.

Goals

- To stop being hypervigilant
- To shrink the inner critic
- To get over toxic shame
- To deconstruct repetition compulsion

Action plans

1. To get over perfectionism

- See that perfectionism is a self-persecutory myth
- You are human and it's normal for you to make mistakes.
- Remind yourself that you make mistakes but mistakes don't make or define you.
- See every mistake as an opportunity to practice loving yourself in a place you've never been loved

2. To get over black and white thinking
   - Reject over-generalized description and judgment.
   - Avoid using 'always', and 'never' to describe yourself.

3. To be more compassionate
   - Don't shame yourself or allow shame to control you.
   - Refuse to be shamed for normal emotional responses like anger, sadness, fear, and depression.
   - Refuse to attack yourself.

4. To stop worrying/obsessing
   - Don't assume or jump into negative details
   - Accept the fact that you can't change the past
   - Forgive your past mistakes.
   - Take this prayer: 'God grant me the serenity to accept the things I cannot change, the courage to change the things I can, and the wisdom to know the difference'.

5. To stop devaluing comparisons to others
   - Say to yourself, 'I wouldn't compare my inside to their outsides'
   - I refuse to be pressured into becoming someone else

6. To disallow guilt
   - That you feel guilty doesn't mean you're guilty
   - Learn to apologize, make amends and let go of your guilt and move on
   - There's no need to apologize over and over again.

7. To use 'should'
   - In place of use 'want to', try 'should'
   - Don't be under any obligation to do what you don't want to.

8. To stop being a workaholic
   - You don't have to always be busy
   - Learn to relax and have fun
   - Don't try to perform 100% of the time

9. To stop judging yourself and others harshly
   - Don't call yourself names
   - Don't allow bullies and critics in your early life to win by agreeing with them
   - Say to yourself: I care for myself. The more solitary, the more friendless, the more unsustained I am, the more I will respect myself.

10. To stop drasticizing/catastrophizing/hypochondriasizing
    - That you are afraid doesn't mean you're in danger
    - Refuse to blow things out of proportion
    - Don't allow yourself to be scared with pictures of your life deteriorating
    - Every pain or ache you feel isn't a story about your imminent demise

11. To stop being negatively focused
    - Stop over-noticing and dwelling on what may be wrong with you or your life
    - Don't discount your minimize your strength and attributes

12. To stop working with time urgency
    - You're not in danger and you have no need to rush

13. To disable every form of performance anxiety
    - Stop procrastinating
    - Don't allow anyone to pressure you with unfair criticism or perfectionist expectations
    - Don't make decisions out of fear

14. To stop perseverating about being attacked
    - Thought-stop your projection of past bullies/critics onto others
    - You are protected by friends and you will be protected by authorities

15. To stop the critic's negative message
    - Remember that you're good enough
    - You're not to blame for the emotional neglect and behavior of your parents or family members
    - Don't allow yourself to be pressured into doing anything
    - Write out a list of positive qualities and accomplishments to read to yourself when you get lost in self-hate.

16. To change your perspective
    Get a journal (preferably a physical one because writing is therapeutic). You can get a journaling app on your phone.
    At the end of the day, list out ten positive things that happened to you each day.

It can be as simple as getting a drink, noticing a color, sitting at the park, or anything at all.

Questions

1. What are the downsides to hypervigilance?
2. How does CPTSD lead to endangerment?
3. Is there anything like normal shame? Is it the same as toxic shame?
4. Why do emotionally abandoned children have a sense of perfectionism?
5. How easy is it for the inner critic to give up its rulership of the psyche easily? How can your healthy ego win against it?
6. How does repetition compulsion help in silencing the inner critic?
7. You meet a child who is emotionally abandoned and traumatized. She is beginning to see the world from this perspective. Why is it important for her to gain perspective-substitution?
8. Why is gratitude difficult but important for anyone who wants to stop living with CPTSD?

CHAPTER 10: SHRINKING THE OUTER CRITIC

Summary

The inner critic is the part of the mind that views you as flawed and unworthy. The outer critic views everyone else as flawed and unworthy. When the outer critic is in charge of your mind, people appear to be too awful and dangerous.

The outer critic alienates us from others by attacking and sending them away so we can build fortresses of isolation whose walls are laundry lists of their exaggerated shortcomings. All it wants to do is protect us from abandonment but it ends us pushing us further into it.

Viewing all relationships through the lens of parental abandonment, the outer critic never lets down its guard. The outer critic transfers unexpressed childhood anger onto others, and silently scapegoats them by blowing current disappointments out of proportion.

Signs of passive aggression:

- Distancing yourself in hurt withdrawal
- Pushing others away with backhanded compliments
- Poor listening hurtful teasing disguised as joking
- Withholding of positive feedback and appreciation
- Chronic lateness
- Poor follow through on commitments

In the guise of honesty, the outer critic can negatively notice only what is imperfect in another. Under the spell of perfectionism, the outer critic can tear the other apart by laundry-listing his normal weakness and foibles.

The inner critic has its own version of excessive honesty which is called 'beating you to the punch'. Afraid of being criticized, the inner critic can launch the survivor into a confession of her every defect in hopes of short-circuiting anyone else from bringing them up.

The outer critic is strong during emotional flashbacks because it transmutes unconscious abandonment pain into an overwhelmingly negative perception of people and of life in general. It obsessively fantasizes, consciously and unconsciously about how people have or could have hurt us.

Over the years, our fantasy of how people have or could have hurt us expands from scary snapshots into film clips and movies of real and imagined betrayals that destroy our capacity to be nurtured by human contact.

Video themes survivors develop in their quest for interpersonal safety:

- Don't trust anyone

- Proud to be a loner
- Better to be alone and safe than to be with backstabbing people
- Lovers always leave you
- Love is wicked
- Kids will only break your heart
- Only fools let on what they really think
- Give them an inch and they'll take a mile

Signs of over-controlling behavior:

- Shaming
- Excessive criticism
- Monologing (controversial control)
- Overall bossiness

Many CPTSD survivors flounder in caustic judgmentalness, shuffling back and forth between pathologizing others (the toxic blame of the outer critic) and pathologizing themselves (the toxic blame of the inner critic.

Scapegoating is the outer critic process whereby personal frustration is unfairly dumped onto others. It is typically fuelled by unworked-through anger about childhood abandonment.

When mindfulness of the critic seems to strengthen it, it's because we are typically flashing back to how our parents rebuked our early protests at their attacks.

When grieving opens into crying, it can release the fear that the outer critic uses to frighten us out of opening up to others. Tears can help us realize that our loneliness is now causing us much unnecessary pain.

Transference is the pipeline from the past that supplies the critic with anger to control, attack, or disapprove of present relationships.

Key takeaways from this chapter

- In CPTSD, the critic can have two aspects: the inner critic and the outer critic.
- The outer critic uses perfectionism and endangerment against others just as the inner critic uses it against yourself.
- The outer critic's arsenal of intimacy-spoiling dynamics must be consciously identified and gradually deactivated.
- Freeze and fight types are polarized to the outer critic. Fawns are dominated by the inner critic. Flights can have the most variance in inner and outer critic ratio.
- The outer critic manifests as passive-aggressiveness by making a habit of silently blaming the wrong person.

- In worse case scenarios, the outer critic drasticizing deteriorates into paranoia which (at its worst) deteriorates into fantasies and delusions of persecution.
- The outer critic forms to remind us that everyone else is surely as dangerous as our original caretakers.
- In the early stage of recovery, the outer critic becomes nastier and stronger when we try to challenge it.
- To shrink the outer critic, you have to use thought substitution. Invoke positive thoughts and images of others to help erode the critic's intimacy-spoiling habit of picking them apart.

Lessons

- The outer critic is the counterpart of the self-esteem destroying inner critic.
- The outer critic rejects others because they are never perfect and they cannot be guaranteed to be safe.
- Perfectionism, in the hands of the outer critic, can be paranoiaclly picayune.
- The outer critic arises most powerfully during emotional flashbacks.
- The degree to which our caretakers attacked or abandoned us for showing vulnerability is the degree to which we later avoid the authentic self-expression that is fundamental to intimacy.
- The outer critic not only scares us from trusting others, but it also pushes us to over-control them to make them safer.
- Many CPTSD survivors get stuck in endless loops of detailing relational inadequacies of others and then of themselves.
- Scapegoating is the reenactment of a parent's abusive role.
- Our recovery depends on us using mindfulness to decrease our habits of dissociation.
- We can use the anger of our grief to energize thought corrections.
- The outer critic displaces anger from the past onto present-day relationships.

Goals

- To identify and gradually deactivate the outer critic
- To stop scapegoating

Action plan

1. To shrink the outer critic
   - Practice mindfulness
   - Focus on positive things around you
2. To renounce outer critic strategies

- Renounce angry criticism of making others afraid of you so you feel safe from them
- Stop the all-or-none/black-and-white thinking. AN example 'why should I bother with people when everyone is so selfish and corrupt'?
- Don't try to micromanage people to prevent them from betraying you
- Don't rant and rave or leave at the first sign of a lonely feeling.
- The fact that you feel lonely even when loved isn't a sign that the other person's love isn't genuine.

3. Practicing thought substitution
- List five recollections of positive interactions with a friend and list five of her attributes.
- Mention a movie, story, or book that was positively written and that helped you. Write out the positivity in it and how you've seen it happen around you.

4. To deal with anger
- When something enrages you, ask yourself what it reminds you of.

Questions

1. How does the outer critic develop?
2. How does the outer critic alienate others from us?
3. How does silencing anger fuel the outer critic's obsession with finding fault and seeing danger in everyone?
4. How does the outer critic use perfectionism to drive others away?
5. How can the thought of relating and socializing drive us into feeling justified in isolation?
6. Why is grieving important?
7. What does the outer critic need to thrive?
8. How does transference work with the outer critic?

CHAPTER 11: GRIEVING

Summary

    1. Grieving

We grieve the losses of childhood because these losses are like the deaths of important parts of ourselves. Effective grieving brings these parts back to life.

Four practices of grieving

- Angering: it diminishes fear and shame
- Crying: the penultimate soothing
- Verbal ventilating: the golden path to intimacy
- Feeling: passively working through grief

If you find that crying or angering is inaccessible, does not help or it makes you feel worse, then your recovery work may need to focus more on deconstructing and shrinking your inner critic.

Grieving aids the survivor immeasurably to work through the death-like experience of being lost and trapped in an emotional flashback. Grieving metabolizes our most painful abandonment feelings, especially those that give rise to suicidal ideation, and at their worst, active suicidality.

The most essential developmental arrests CPTSD survivors suffer

- Deaths of our self-compassion
- Death of our self-esteem
- Death of our abilities to protect ourselves
- Death of fully expressing ourselves
- Death of the absence of parental care

With sufficient grieving, a survivor realizes that she was innocent and loveable as a child. By mourning the bad luck of not being born to loving parents, the survivor finds within herself a fierce, unshakeable self-allegiance. She becomes ready, willing, and able to be there for herself no matter what she is experiencing internally or externally.

Once the critic has been sufficiently diminished and once thought-correction techniques have made the psyche more user-friendly, a person begins to tap into grief's sweet relief-granting potential. He learns to grieve in a way that promotes and enhances compassion for the abandoned child he was and for the survivor he is today.

Common anger-powered critic attacks:

- Why did I ask such a stupid question?
- Could I have had an uglier expression on my face?
- Who am I kidding?

- How could an undeserving loser like me wish for love?
- No wonder I feel like shit, I am a piece of shit

2. Crying

Crying and angering are the two key emotional tools for releasing the pain of the abandonment mélange.

3. Verbal ventilation

This is speaking or writing in a manner that airs out and releases painful feelings.

Verbal ventilating from the self-attacking or drasticizing perspective of the critic isn't effective grieving. It triggers or intensifies flashbacks which lead to self and intimacy-injuring behavior.

4. Feelings

Feeling is a subtler, passive process than emoting. Emoting is when we cry, anger out, or verbally ventilate the energy of an inner emotional experience. Feeling, on the other hand, is the inactive process of staying present to internal emotional experience without reacting.

Key takeaways from this chapter

Grieving is the key process for working through the host of losses that come from growing up in a CPTSD-inducing family.

Grieving supports recovery from the many painful, deathlike losses caused by childhood traumatization.

A survivor can grieve herself out of

- Fear: the death of feeling safe
- Shame: the death of feeling worthy
- Depression: the death of feeling fully alive

Grieving can move you out of the extreme combination of fear, shame, and depression that is at the emotional core of flashbacks. It releases you from the impatience and frustration that can arise when monster flashbacks bully you into giving up. Anger and crying can rescue you from this.

Over time, anger also becomes fuel for the critic and actually exacerbates fear by creating an increasingly dangerous internal environment. Anything the survivor says, thinks, feels, imagines, or wishes for is subjected to an intimidating inner attack.

Benefits of angering

- It is therapeutic

- It allows the survivor to turn anger away from herself and defend herself against unjust attacks
- It rescues the survivor from toxic shame
- It redirects blame back to where it belongs
- It augments the survivor's motivation to keep fighting to establish internal boundaries against the critic
- It serves to rescue a person from the childlike sense of powerlessness that she is flashing back to.
- It antidotes fear while reawakening and nurturing the instinct of self-preservation
- It builds a sense of outer and inner boundaries which keeps the survivor safe from the bullying of others and the inner critic
- It empowers the myriad thought corrections and substitutions needed to establish the survivor's belief in her own essential goodness and in the lovability of discriminately chosen others.

Benefits of crying

- It is therapeutic
- It awakens our developmentally arrested instinct of self-compassion which leads to building self-esteem while disabling the self-abandonment that leads to flashbacks.

Verbal ventilation is therapeutic to the degree that a person's words are colored by and descriptive of the anger, sadness, fear, shame, and/or depression she feels. Ventilation that is liberally punctuated with actual crying or angering is powerful.

Benefits of verbal ventilation

- It fosters the recoveree's ability to put words to feelings and ultimately to accurately interpret and communicate about his various feeling states. When this is repeated consistently, new neural pathways grow that allow the left and right brain to work together so that the person can actually think and feel at the same time.
- It helps the recoveree think about feeling states in a way that creates healthy, helpful, and appropriate responses to feelings.
- It promotes the same type of fear-release and shame dissolution as angering and crying but also helps to expose the manifold guises of the critic's self-attack and fear-arousal programs.
- It helps us identify and communicate about needs that have long been unmet because of our childhood abandonment.
- It is the key way to make friends.
- Reciprocal verbal ventilation is the highway to intimacy in adult relationships

Feeling is a kinesthetic experience. It is the process of shifting the focus of your awareness off of thinking and onto your affects, energetic states, and sensations. Feeling involves consciously reversing the learned survival mechanism of clamping down on pain to banish it from awareness.

Benefits of feeling

- It can heal digestive problems
- It helps you grieve out

Lessons

- Grieving is an irreplaceable tool for resolving the overwhelming feelings that arise during emotional flashbacks.
- The greatest hindrance to effective grieving is the inner critic.
- A good cry from grief has the ability to restore a person's inner strength.
- Fear drives the toxic inner critic.
- Self-hate is the most grievous reenactment of parental abandonment.
- As you become better at grieving, you will notice that your critic's volume and intensity ebbs dramatically.
- The ability to say no is the backbone of our instinct of self-protection.
- Tears release fear. It can sometimes be the only process that will resolve a flashback.
- When we speak from what we feel, language is imbued with emotion, and pain can be released through what we say, think, or write.
- Feeling occurs when we direct our attention to an emotionally or physically painful state and surrender to this experience without resistance.

Goals

- To grieve childhood losses
- To re-parent yourself

Action plans

1. To give yourself verbal nurturance
   - Give yourself a generous amount of praise and positive feedback
   - Be willing to entertain questions
   - Encourage yourself with positive words

2. To give yourself spiritual nurturance
   - Have fun
   - Look at your strengths and tell yourself what you're worth
   - Sing your favorite song while you're in the shower

- Get yourself a gift and write a loving note to yourself
- Go out to the park, take a vacation, or go to a place where you see the beauty in nature
- Paint, draw and sing

3. To get emotional nurturance
   - Release your anger in a way that doesn't hurt anyone
   - Be generous in giving yourself love, warmth, tenderness, and compassion
   - Allow yourself to cry
   - Tell yourself you're safe and no one will hurt you.

4. To get physical nurturance
   - Eat healthy meals
   - Sleep at the right time
   - Take care of yourself
   - Try out new hobbies you always thought of as a child

5. To get over fear
   - Allow yourself to cry and get angry
   - Cry for the child who was not appreciated and reflected as special, worthy, and easy to love.

6. Allow yourself to grieve (without anger and tears)
   - Focus on your breathing
   - Take deep, slow, and rhythmic breathing stretches. Take a deep breath and count 1-10 before releasing the breath slowly
   - Spend time journaling about how you feel

7. Verbal ventilating
   - Speak up about how you feel. Don't detach your emotions from your words.
   - Speak out about how you feel when you're alone and no one can hear you.

8. To feel your feelings
   - Think back to a time you felt abandoned
   - Comfort your younger self. Tell your younger self you can feel her pain from feeling abandoned at that time and that she had to go through it alone and it never should have happened to you.
   - Tell yourself you want to comfort her and hold it because she didn't deserve it. Tell her how much you love her and will continue to love her.

9. To gain healing
    - Look for a safe place where you wouldn't be heard (for this practice).
    - Close your eyes and remember a time you felt compassionate towards someone.
    - Invoke self-compassion via a memory of someone who was kind to you or someone being kind to you.
    - Verbally ventilate about what is bothering you (you can do this in a journal or say it out).
    - Imagine yourself being comforted by a higher power.
    - Remember a time when you felt better from crying or angering or seeing someone else cry.
    - Remember a time when being angry or when someone else being angry, saved you from harm.
    - Imagine your anger forming a protective fiery shield around you
    - Imagine your tears or anger carrying any fear, shame, or depression up and out of you.
    - Imagine that you're holding your inner child compassionately. Tell her it's normal to be sad or get mad from feeling hurt or bad. Tell her you'll protect her from being criticized.
    - Practice deep breaths. Take it in slowly and release it slowly
    - Play evocative music
    - Watch a movie that portrays enviable anger release.

Questions
1. Why is grieving important to CPTSD survivors?
2. When is the right time to stop grieving? What signs should you look at for in yourself?
3. Why is anger good for a CPTSD survivor? How can it be therapeutic?
4. What is the difference between crying and dysfunctional whining?

CHAPTER 12: THE MAP: MANAGING THE ABANDONMENT DEPRESSION

Summary

CPTSD survivors experience cycles of reactivity that incites fear, shame, and panicky inner critic thinking which in turn lead to an adrenalized 4F trauma response. Here's how it works.

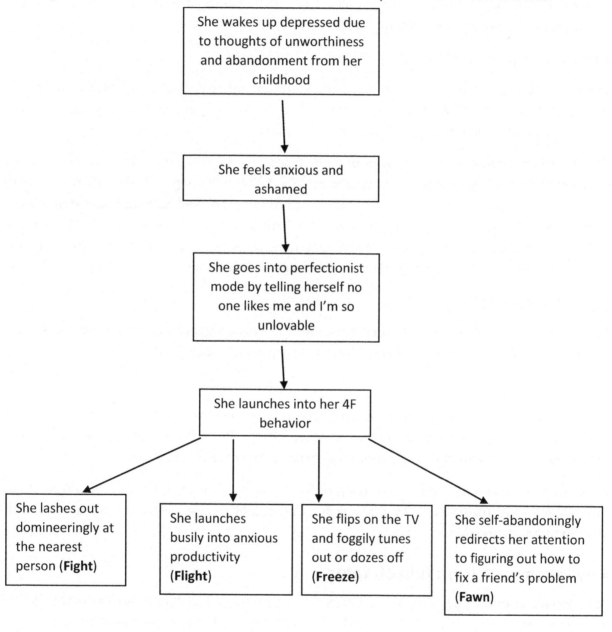

This dynamics of the cycles of reactivity works in reverse during early recovery when survivors notice they've slipped back into a dysfunctional 4F behavior. It triggers new self-attacking criticism and then leads to further fear, shame and increases abandonment depression.

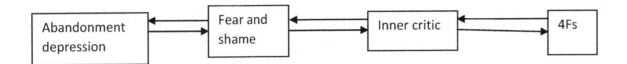

When we are triggered and lost in a 4F response, we fight, flee, freeze or fawn to dissociate ourselves from the painful voice of the critic. On a deeper level, the critic is distracting and dissociating us from our emotional pain. Fear and shame also dissociate us from the abandonment depression which is the bottom layer.

Abandonment Depression

When our abandonment depression is unpremeditated, either kind of tiredness can trigger us into fear. This then activates the inner critic which then translates 'tired' into 'endangering imperfection' which in turn triggers us into a 4F response.

The cyclothymic two-step is the dance of flight types or subtypes who habitually overreact to their tiredness with workaholic or busyholic activity. Self-medicating with their own adrenalin, they 'run' to counteract the emotional tiredness of the unprocessed abandonment depression. They exhaust themselves physically, and become temporarily too depleted or sick to continue running then they collapse into an accumulated depression so painful that they re-launch desperately into flight speed at the first sign of replenished adrenalin.

How to Manage Emotional Tiredness

Focus inside to see if you have flashed back into the abandonment depression whenever you experience a HALT feeling. HALT means Hungry, Angry, Lonely, and Tired.

Recovery

Recovery is to a large extent progressive. It begins on the cognitive level when psychoeducation and mindfulness help us understand that we have CPTSD. This helps us learn how to approach the journey of deconstructing the various life-spoiling dynamics of CPTSD.

It also involves shrinking the critic, grieving childhood losses (which can last for years), working through fear and toxic shame by grieving for the loss of our self-esteem, and dealing with abandonment depression.

Key takeaways from this chapter

Abandoning parents respond to their children with anger, disgust, or further abandonment which in turn exacerbates the fear, shame, and despair that become the abandonment mélange.

Ending our reactivity to depression is a long and difficult journey

When depression is most helpful, it gives us access to a unique spring of intuition such as that which informs us that something we once valued is no longer useful. Change in this situation can lead to depression.

Benefits of Mindfulness:

It allows us to stay acceptingly open to our emotional, visceral, and somatic experiences without retreating into the cycle of reactivity.

It allows us to stay present with the physical sensations of fearful hyperarousal.

Signs of fear

- Muscular tightness or tension anywhere in the body especially the alimentary canal
- Tension in the jaw, throat, chest, diaphragm or belly
- Nausea
- Jumpiness
- Feeling tired
- Shortness of breath
- Hyperventilation
- Alimentary distress.

Signs of hypo-aroused sensations

- Heaviness
- Swollenesss
- Exhaustion
- Emptiness
- Hunger
- Longing
- Soreness
- Deadness

Feelings of abandonment commonly masquerade as the psychological sensations of hunger. Hunger pain soon after a big meal is rarely truly about food; it is camouflaged emotional hunger and the longing for a safe, nurturing connection.

Emotional tiredness comes from not resting enough in a safe relationship with yourself or with another.

Lessons

- Mindfulness helps us metabolize the fear and shame that we were forced to feel about being depressed.

- Depression is sometimes an invaluable herald to the need to slow down for rest and restoration.
- Overreaction to depression reinforces toxic shame.
- Mindful merging with the subtle emotions and sensations of depression is the finishing tool of deconstructing self-abandonment.
- When the critic is especially loud and persistent, shifting awareness from thinking to feeling your sensations is a potent way of coming home to a safer place.
- Food cannot satiate the hunger pain of abandonment, only loving support can.
- Food addictions are difficult to manage because the food was the first source of self-comforting that was available to us.
- It is possible that all addictive behavior is our misguided attempts to self-medicate deeper abandonment pain and unmet attachment needs.
- Sometimes feeling tired isn't a sign of sleep deprivation but an emotional experience of the abandonment depression.
- Emotional exhaustion masquerades as physiological tiredness.

Goals

- To deconstruct self-abandonment
- To distinguish between depressed thinking and depressed feeling

Action Plans

1. To deconstruct self-abandonment
   Practice mindfulness
2. To identify emotional pain
   Be sure of what you feel.
   When you feel hunger pangs after eating or when you're bored, practice mindfulness instead.
   When you're tired practice mindfulness

Questions

1. Is there any benefit or none linked with dissociation?
2. Why is it important to stay mindful as we recover when the cycle of reactivity hits?
3. What are the downsides to chronic emotional abandonment of a child?
4. What's the difference between depressed thinking and depressed feeling?
5. Why is sensate focusing important?
6. What are the benefits associated with somatic mindfulness?
7. How can you differentiate between physical hunger and emotional hunger?

CHAPTER 13: A RELATIONAL APPROACH TO HEALING ABANDONMENT

Summary

The therapist

Healing our attachment disorders usually requires a reparative relational experience with a therapist, partner, or trusted friend who is able to remain compassionately present to their own painful and dysphoric feelings. It is essential that CPTSD survivors are comfortable feeling and expressing their sadness, anger, fear, shame, and depression.

Safe and empathic eye and voice connection with a therapist who has good enough emotional intelligence models to the client on how to stay acceptingly present to all her own affects.

Many CPTSD survivors have never had a safe enough relationship and the therapist is the first they'll establish such a relationship with.

Clients need to feel safe enough with the therapist to describe their humiliation and overwhelm. The therapist needs to be nurturing enough to provide the empathy and calm support that was missing in the client's early experience.

The therapist needs to be able to tolerate and work therapeutically with the sudden evaporation of trust that is characteristic of CPTSD

Key qualities of relating that are essential to the development of trust

- Empathy: without this, a therapist triggers the sense of danger and abandonment in clients
- Authentic vulnerability: relationship makes healthy relationship
- Dialogicality
- Corroborative relationship repair

Emotional reflection requires the therapist to be emotionally vulnerable and reveal that he also gets mad, sad, bad and scared sometimes. It shows the client the value of being vulnerable and encourages her to risk wading into her own vulnerability.

Guidelines for self-disclosure:

- Use it sparingly
- Use it primarily to promote a matrix of safety and trust in the relationship.
- Avoid sharing vulnerabilities that are currently raw and unintegrated.
- Don't disclose in order to work through your personal stuff or to meet your personal narcissistic need for verbal ventilation or personal edification.

- You can share your appreciation or be touched by a client's attempt or focus on or soothe your vulnerabilities, it's best not to accept the offer.

Dialogicality

Dialogicality develops out of a teamwork approach, which is a mutual brainstorming about the client's issues and concerns. This leads to a full exploration of ambivalences, conflicts, and other life difficulties.

It energizes both participants in a conversation and implies respectful mutuality.

It is enhanced when the therapist offers feedback from a take-it-or-leave-it stance

Dialogicality and the 4Fs

Fight	Flight	Freeze	Fawn
Dodges real intimacy with her talking defensively.	More dialogical than other types. She can obsess about 'safe' abstract concerns that are quite removed from her deeper issues	Needs to be encouraged to discover and talk about her experience	Uses listening to encourage the therapist to do too much of the talking.
Therapy can be counterproductive for these types because months or years of uninterrupted monologing in sessions exacerbate their sense of entitlement	Therapist needs to steer her into her deeper emotionally based concerns to help her learn a more intimacy-enhancing dialogicality	Can get lost in superficial and barely relevant free associations as she struggles to learn to talk about herself.	May hide herself in listening and eliciting defense to avoid the scary work of gradually insinuating herself into the relationship and nudging it towards dialogicality
		She needs to see that emotionally disconnected talking is an old childhood habit that was meant to keep her buoyant above her undealt-with emotional pain.	

Corroborative rapport repair is the process by which relationships recover and grow closer from successful conflict resolution. It is the most transformative, intimacy-building process that a therapist can model.

Interviewing your therapist

- Interviewing your therapist is to ascertain whether your potential therapist is able and willing to work with empathy, authentic vulnerability, dialogicality, and corroborative rapport repair.
- A suitable therapist should be able to answer your question about their approach and generally talk with you on the phone for at least five minutes before scheduling a meeting. If the therapist responds to you in an aloof, critical, or shaming way, you need to look for another therapist.
- You can ask a prospective therapist if they've done their therapy.

Co-counseling

- If you can't find a good enough therapist, and /or if you want to supplement your current therapy, you can get a safe partner who is willing to work with you to mutually evolve a co-counseling relationship.
- Meet weekly and practice 30 to 60 minutes sessions
- The counselee begins by talking about his or her concerns with the counselor while the counselor practices active listening.
- Mirroring occurs when we repeat keywords or phrases that the other person says to let them know that we are paying attention to them.
- Open-ended questions are the penultimate active listening technique

Websites where you can find an online or live support group:

www.outofthefog.website

www.ptsdforum.org

www.coda.org (for fawn types or subtypes)

www.ascasupport.org (for childhood abuse survivors)

www.adultchildren.org (for adult children of alcoholics)

www.siawso.org (survivors of incest)

www.thehotline.org (survivors of childhood abuse that became victims of domestic violence)

www.nobully.com (survivors who due to repetition compulsion or bad luck are stuck in a job or relationship where they are bullied)

www.daughtersofnarcissisticmothers.com (survivors of narcissistic moms)

Key takeaways from this chapter

- Co-regulation of affects promotes the development of the inner neural circularity necessary to metabolize overwhelmingly painful feelings.
- Emotional flashback management is empowered when it is taught in the context of a safe relationship.
- Empathy involves immersing yourself in another's psychological state by feeling yourself into the other's experience.
- The degree to which a therapist attunes to and welcomes all of the client's experience, to that same degree can the client learn to welcome it in her or himself.
- Authentic vulnerability often begins with emotionally reverberating with the client.
- The therapist's use of emotional self-disclosure helps the client move out of the slippery, shame-lined pit of emotional perfectionism.
- Dialogicality occurs when two conversing people move fluidly and interchangeably between speaking (an aspect of healthy narcissism) and listening (an aspect of healthy codependence). It prevents either person from polarizing to a dysfunctional narcissistic or codependent type of relating.
- Practice therapeutic confidentiality. Let what is said in a session stay in the session.

Lessons

- Those with CPTSD-spawned attachment disorders never learn the communication skills that engender closeness and a sense of belonging. When it comes to relating, they are plagued by debilitating social anxiety and social phobia when they are at the severe end of the continuum of CPTSD.
- Empathy deepens via careful listening and full elicitation of the client's experience along with the time-honored techniques of mirroring and paraphrasing which show the client the degree to which we get him.
- Self-empathy or self-acceptance is one of the packages that come with empathy.
- Vulnerability is offered primarily to normalize and de-shame the inexorable, existential imperfection of the human condition.
- Self-disclosure is powerful enough to heal shame and cultivate hope.
- One of the most common reasons clients terminate prematurely is the gradual accumulation of dissatisfactions that they do not feel safe enough to bring up or talk about.
- Helping survivors out of the abyss of emotional flashbacks is a necessary form of rescuing. A key place to practice healthy rescuing is in the realm of the critic.

Goals

- To help the client feel safe
- To find a good therapist

Action plans

1. To connect with your client
   - Practice active listening when you're with your client
   - Share a simple story of something that happened to you that's similar and connects with your client's story to aid vulnerability
   - Speak words that resonate with your client: 'I understand your pain. I felt this way with my parents when growing up' is an example of what you can say
   - Engage in dialogicality
   - Gain psychoeducation

2. To build rapport repair or conflict resolution with clients
   - Identify the misattunement
   - Model vulnerability and own your part in a conflict

Questions

1. Why does sharing a story with a client show empathy?
2. What ways can you show empathy so your patients can connect with you?
3. What are the benefits associated with dialogicality?
4. Why is extensive dialogicality inappropriate in the early stages of therapy?
5. What's the worst form of therapeutic neglect?

CHAPTER 14: FORGIVENESS: BEGIN WITH THE SELF

Summary

Forgiving isn't a black-and-white thing. If you decide to forgive abuses that you haven't fully grieved or abuses that are still occurring or heinous abuses that shouldn't be forgiven, you may get stuck and not fully recover.

Premature forgiveness

- Premature forgiveness mimics the defenses of denial and repression. It keeps unprocessed feelings of anger and hurt about childhood trauma out of awareness.
- It prevents the inner child from being rightfully angry about her parents' cold-hearted abandonment of her. She wouldn't be able to express and release those old angry feelings.
- It prohibits the survivor from reconnecting with her instinctual self-protectiveness. She may never learn to use her anger to stop present-day unfairness.

When we learn to effectively grieve through present-day hurts, we quite naturally move back to loving feelings.

Key takeaways from this chapter

- The possibility of attaining real feelings of forgiveness is usually lost when there is a premature, cognitive decision to forgive.
- When forgiveness has substance it is felt palpably in the heart and it is usually an extension of the emotion of compassion.
- Compassion isn't forgiveness but through it, forgiveness is born.
- Forgiveness is a feeling. It can never be complete, permanent, or a done deal.
- When we thoroughly vent our angry feelings about the past, feelings of forgiveness become more accessible. When we learn how to grieve ourselves out of abandonment flashbacks, we reemerge into a feeling of belonging to and loving the world.

Lessons

- Just like healing and recovery, forgiveness is a process.
- Without effective grieving of trauma, abandonment, and abuse, forgiveness can't be attained.
- Forgiveness cannot be forced.
- Forgiveness like love and other emotions is a human feeling experience that is temporarily ours.

Goals

- To forgive

Action plan

1. To forgive
- Acknowledge the full weight of all that has been done to you
- Grieve it
- See from another person's point of view. How did your abuser grow up? What made your abuser who she is?
- Remember that forgiveness is for your peace not for the abuser.
- Forgiving doesn't change the past but it enlarges the future – Paul Boose

Questions

1. How do you differentiate between real forgiveness and premature forgiveness?
2. What's the difference between forgiveness and compassion?
3. Why is grieving important to forgiveness?

CHAPTER 15: BIBLIOTHERAPY AND THE COMMUNITY OF BOOKS

Summary

Bibliotheraphy is a term that describes the very real process of being positively and therapeutically influenced by what you read.

Benefits of bibliotheraphy

- It rescues you from the common CPTSD feeling of abject isolation and alienation
- It enhances CPTSD recovery.

Recommended reading

Author	Book	Purpose/ who should read this book
Alice Miller	The drama of the gifted child	1. Those who want to overcome denial and understand the profound impact of poor parenting. 2. For fawn types
Gravitz and Bowden	Guide to recovery	1. Oriented to recovering from having alcoholic parents 2. Relevant for those who had traumatizing parents
L.Davis and E.Bass	The courage to heal	1. For recovery from sexual abuse
Jack Kornfield	A path with heart	1. For those using medication to increase self-compassion
Steven Levine	Who dies	1. To aid those who want to increase mindful and radical acceptance
Sue Johnson	Hold Me Tight (Book and DVD)	1. For couples who want to use emotional vulnerability to develop real intimacy and a healthy attachment bond.
John Bradshaw	Healing the shame that binds	1. For those recovering from toxic shame and growing up in a dysfunctional family
Judith Herman	Trauma and recovery	1. For recovery from CPTSD
Susan Anderson	The journey from abandonment to healing	1. For recovery from divorce 2. CPTSD recovery

J. Middleton-Moz	Children of trauma	1. For recovery
Beverly Engel	Healing your emotional self	1. Advocates angering-at-the-critic work
Theodore Rubin	Compassion and self-hate	1. To those who want to appeal to self-compassion
Susan Forward	Betrayal of Innocence	1. To those who want to find recovery
Bryan Brown	Soul without shame	For those who want to shrink the inner critic via angering at the critic and mindfulness
Susan Vaughan	The talking cure	1. For those who want to understand how therapy and relational healing works with very accessible neuroscientific evidence and an enlightened view of therapy
Lewis and Amini	A general theory of love	1. Accessible poetic and scientific argument on the human need for love and attachment.
Pat Love	The emotional incest syndrome	1. Great book to heal from codependence entrapment
Robin Norwood	Women who love too much	1. Early classic on Codependence
Gay Hendricks, Lucia Capacchione	Learning to love yourself recovery of your inner child	1. Aids journaltheraphy
Cheri Huber	There is nothing wrong with you	1. To those who want to overcome shame and cultivate self-compassion
Christine Lawson	Understanding the borderline mother	1. To those healing from having a borderline or narcissistic mother
Elan Golomb	Trapped in the mirror	1. To those healing from a narcissistic parent
John Gottman	The seven principles of making marriage work	1. For those who want to make their marriage work

Key takeaways from this chapter

Augmenting therapy with journaling about your cognitive and emotional responses to what you've read enhances recovery.

Lessons

- At its best, bibliotheraphy is also relational healing.

Goals

- To journal
- To gain psychoeducation

Action plans

1. To journal
- A personal journal is an ideal environment in which to become. It is a perfect place for you to think, feel, discover, expand, remember and dream – Brad Wilcox
- Use your journal to unleash all the anger, pain, joy, and emotion inside of you.

Questions

1. What are the benefits of bibliotheraphy?

2. What is your take on journaling? Do you think it's an effective way to process your feelings? Do you think it's more of a childish hobby?

3. Does the thought of putting your emotions and feelings into words scare you? Yes? No?

4. If you answered yes to question 3, why?

CHAPTER 16: SELF-HELP TOOLS

Summary

How to know you're recovering

- You're increasing mindfulness which decreases your unconscious 4F acting out
- Your critic shrinks
- Your brain becomes more user-friendly
- Grieving your childhood losses builds your emotional intelligence
- Your body relaxes and your mind becomes more peaceful
- Your healthy ego matures into a healthy sense of self
- Your life narrative becomes self-compassion and self-affirming
- Your emotional vulnerability creates authentic experiences of intimacy
- You attain a good enough safe relationship

Timeout

- Things said in the heat of a flashback can wound deeply and engrave themselves in the psyche of the other in ways that cripple trust. So much of this needless intimacy-destruction will be prevented if both members of the couple agree that either of them can call a timeout whenever they feel too triggered to be lovingly confrontive, or are experiencing the other as flashing back into being overly aggressive.
- Timeouts can range from one minute to 24 hours depending on how long it takes either or both partners to achieve good flashback management
- Timeouts work best when the person calling them nominates a time to resume conflict resolution so that timeouts do not become techniques for dodging issues.
- A timeout can be used individually as a time to release any accumulated charge.

Key takeaways from this chapter

The attacks of the critic often operate below the radar of self-awareness. Unless we identify them, we are at their mercy and helpless to deconstruct them. Once we learn to recognize inner critic attacks, the simple techniques of thought-stopping and thought-substitution are powerful tools for short-circuiting the critic.

Two of the most common reasons that relationships break up are irreconcilable differences and irreparable damages. The latter could have been prevented in many cases if couples knew how to use timeouts judiciously.

Transference

Is often a type of flashback whereby we unconsciously react to our significant others as though they were our childhood caretakers. When this occurs we displace onto them a great deal of our unresolved childhood emotional pain.

Truly healing resolutions to conflict typically occur when each partner owns their part and expresses an apology for their contribution to the conflict.

Lessons

- Perfectionism attacks are fueled by toxic shame, and create chronic self-hate and self-flagellation.
- Endangerment attacks fueled by fear, create chronic hypervigilance and anxiety.
- Two of the most common reasons that relationships break up are irreconcilable differences and irreparable damages. The latter could have been prevented in many cases if couples knew how to use timeouts judiciously.

Goals

- To become better by using all self-help tools

Action plans

To use all the toolboxes

Toolbox 1

Tick the box that appeals to you

I want to develop a more constantly loving and accepting relationship with myself. I want an increasing capacity for self-acceptance	
I want to learn to become the best possible friend to myself.	
I want to attract, into my life, relationships that are based on love, respect, fairness, and mutual support.	
I want to uncover full, uninhibited self-expression	
I want to attain the best possible physical health	
I want to cultivate a balance of vitality and peace	
I want to attract, to myself, loving friends, and a loving community.	
I want increasing freedom from toxic shame	

I want increasing freedom from unnecessary fear.	
I want rewarding and fulfilling work	
I want a fair amount of peace of mind, spirit, soul, and body.	
I want to increase my capacity to play and have fun	
I want to make plenty of room for beauty and nature in my life.	
I want sufficient physical and monetary resources	
I want a fair amount of help (self, human, or divine) to get what I need.	
I want God's love grace and blessing	
I want a balance of loving interaction and healthy self-sufficiency	
I want full emotional expression with a balance of laughter and tears	
I want a sense of meaningfulness and fulfillment	
I want to find effective and non-abusive ways to deal with anger	
I want all this for each and every other being	

Toolbox 2

Guidelines for fairness and intimacy

Tick the box that appeals to you

0I have a right to be treated with respect	
I have the right to say no	
I have the right to make mistakes	
I have the right to reject unsolicited advice or feedback	
I have the right to negotiate for change	
I have the right to change my mind or my plans	
I have a right to change my circumstances or course of action	
I have the right to have my own feelings, beliefs, opinions, preferences, etc	
I have the right to protest sarcasm, destructive criticism, or unfair treatment.	

I have a right to refuse to take responsibility for anyone else's problems.	
I have a right to refuse to take responsibility for anyone's bad behavior.	
I have a right to play, waste time, and not always be productive	
I have a right to occasionally be childlike and immature	
I have a right to complain about life's unfairness and injustices	
I have a right to occasionally be irrational in safe ways	
I have a right to seek healthy and mutually supportive relationships	
I have a right to ask friends for a modicum of help and emotional support	
I have a right to complain and verbally ventilate in moderation	
I have a right to grow, evolve and prosper	

Toolbox 3

Suggested internal responses to common critic attacks

Perfectionism attacks

Perfectionism: I do not have to be perfect to be safe or loved in the present. I'm letting go of relationships that require perfection. I have a right to make mistakes. My mistakes do not make me a mistake. Every mistake or mishap is an opportunity to practice loving myself in the places I have never been loved.

All-or-none and black-and-white thinking: I reject extreme or over-generalized descriptions, judgments, or criticisms. Statements that describe me as "always," "never," "this or that" are grossly inaccurate.

Self-hate, self-disgust, and toxic shame: I'm on my side, I'm a good enough person, I refuse to trash myself or turn to shame or anyone that shames me.

Micromanagement/worrying/obsessing/looping: I will not repetitively examine details over and over. I would forgive my past mistakes, I will not second guess myself or control the uncontrollable. I will not micromanage myself or others

Unfair/devaluing comparisons: I refuse to compare myself unfavorably to others. I will not judge myself for not being at peak performance all the time.

Guilt: Feeling guilty doesn't mean I'm guilty. I refuse to make decisions and choices out of guilt. Sometimes I need to feel the guilt and do it anyway. I am no longer a victim and I will not accept unfair blame.

Shoulding: I will substitute the words 'want to' for 'should' and only follow this imperative if I want to.

Over-productivity/workaholism/busy-holism: I'm a human being, not a human doing. I choose not to be perpetually productive. I subscribe to vacillating along a continuum of efficiency.

Harsh judgments of self and others/name-calling: I refuse to let bullies and critics of my early life win by joining and agreeing with them. I refuse to attack myself or others. I care for myself.

Endangerment attacks

Drasticizing/catastrophizing/hypochondriasizing: I may feel afraid but I am not in danger. I am not in trouble with my parents. I refuse to scare myself with thoughts and pictures of my life deteriorating.

Negative focus: I will not anxiously look for or dwell on what might go wrong or what might be wrong with me. I will notice, visualize and enumerate my accomplishment, talents, and qualities.

Time urgency: I am not in danger and I do not need to rush. I will not hurry unless it is a true emergency.

Disabling performance anxiety: I am reducing procrastination by reminding myself not to accept unfair criticism or perfectionist expectations from anyone

Perseverating about being attacked: I will thought-stop my projection of past bullies/critics unto others. The majority of my fellow human beings are peaceful people. I invoke thoughts and images of my friends' love and support.

Toolbox 4

Tools for lovingly resolving conflict

1. Normalize the inevitability of conflict and establish a safe forum for it
2. The goal is to inform and negotiate for change not punish
3. Imagine how it would be easiest to hear about your grievance from another person and say it in the easiest way for you to hear.
4. Preface complaints with acknowledgment of the good of the other and your mutual relationship.
5. No name-calling, sarcasm, or character assassination
6. No analyzing the other or mind-reading
7. No interrupting or filibustering
8. Be dialogical

9. No denial of the other's rights
10. Be willing to agree to differ
11. Avoid 'you' statements. Use 'I' statements that identify your feelings and your experiences of what you perceive as unfair
12. Ask yourself what hurts the most to try to find your key complaint
13. Stick to the issue until both persons feel fully heard
14. Present a complaint as lovingly and as calmly as possible
15. Take timeouts if a discussion becomes heated
16. Discharge as much of any accumulated charge beforehand as possible
17. Own responsibility for any accumulated charge in the anger that might come from not talking about it soon enough
18. Own responsibility for accumulated charge displaced from other hurts
19. Commit to growing in your understanding of how much of your charge comes from childhood abuse/neglect
20. Commit to recovering from the losses of childhood by effectively identifying, grieving, and reclaiming them
21. Apologize from an unashamed place.

Toolbox 5

Self gratitude

Write out 12 entries for each category. Write out the good things about yourself. You can get someone to help you. See it as a unique selling point for yourself.

Self-gratitude	Gratitude about others
Accomplishments	Friends (past and current)
Traits	Inspiring people
Good deeds	Inspiring authors
Peak experiences	School friends (whether or not you're still in contact)
Life enjoyments	Circles of friends (past and current)
Intentions	Childhood friends (you do not need to still be in touch with them
Good habits	Teachers
Jobs	Kindness of strangers
Subjects studied	Pets and animals
Obstacles overcome	Work friends (past and current)
Grace received	Groups (past and current)
Nurturing memories	Nurturing memories

Toolbox 6

13 steps for managing flashbacks

1. Say to yourself: I'm having a flashback
2. Remind yourself: I feel afraid but I am not in danger
3. Own your right/need to have boundaries
4. Speak reassuringly to the inner child
5. Deconstruct eternity thinking
6. Remind yourself that you are in an adult body
7. Ease back into your body
- Gently ask your body to relax
- Breathe deeply and slowly
- Slow down
- Find a safe place
- Feel the fear in your body without reacting to it
8. Resist the inner critic's drasticizing and catastrophizing
- Use thought-stopping to halt the critic
- Use thought substitution and thought correction to replace negative thinking
9. Allow yourself to grieve
10. Cultivate safe relationships and seek support
11. Learn to identify flashbacks
12. Figure out what you're flashing back to
13. Be patient with a slow recovery process

Questions

1. Why is timeout important during conflict?
2. What is transference and why can it be dangerous?